At the Trucking Company

Illustrations

Penny Dann

Picture Credits

© Bette. S. Garber/Highway Images: 8, 26
© Charles Thatcher/Tony Stone Images: 22
© David J. Sams/Tony Stone Images: 28
© David Shultz/Tony Stone Worldwide: 30
© Don Spiro/Tony Stone Images: cover
© 1994 Gary Bublitz/Dembinsky Photo Assoc. Inc: 4
© Gary Hayes/Tony Stone Images: 14
© Jack McConnell: 3, 6, 10, 16, 18, 20, 24
© Jon Riley/Tony Stone Worldwide: 12

Library of Congress Cataloging-in-Publication Data

Greene, Carol.

At the trucking company / by Carol Greene.
p.   cm.
Summary: In simple text, explains what happens
at a trucking company, who works there,
and the special machines truckers use to do their jobs.
ISBN 1-56766-564-0 (lib. bdg. : alk. paper)
1. Trucking—United States—Juvenile literature.
2. Truck drivers—United States—Juvenile literature.
3. Occupations.
[1. Trucking. 2. Occupations.]   I. Title.

HE5623.G73   1998   98-13472
388.3'24'0973—dc21   CIP
                                        AC

At the

Trucking Company

By Carol Greene

The Child's World®, Inc.

SLAM! THUD! VROOM!

This trucking company is a big place. Some people are driving big trucks. Others are unloading what's inside them.

This company is a **common carrier**. That means it moves things from one place to another. Each driver usually goes to the same place on the same days.

Common carriers move all kinds of things.

Most trucking companies work for other companies. They move many different things. Trucks might move farm equipment, or cars, or food, or material for making clothes.

This truck is moving new boats to a warehouse.

CLICK! RUSTLE. RUSTLE.

Traffic clerks have a big job. They must check all of the things that the trucks will move today.

Traffic clerks have very important jobs.

How much does each thing weigh? How much money does it cost? Where does it have to go?

CLICK. CLICK.

The traffic clerks and their helpers put all of these facts into a computer.

Shipping clerks make sure the right things go onto the right trucks.

They make sure that the right things are going to the right places, too.

THUD! THUD!

Freight handlers load the goods into the trucks. They are strong people.

But sometimes the goods are just too heavy to lift. Then the freight handlers use machines to help them.

The forklift is one machine that helps freight handlers.

Terminal managers tell the freight handlers what to do. The managers must make sure all the freight gets loaded onto the right trucks.

The terminal is the big building where the trucks are kept.

RUSTLE!

Dispatchers tell each driver which truck to drive. They make sure the right things are on the right truck, too. They see that everything gets done on time.

The dispatcher is very important.

The director of operations is in charge of everyone else. The director makes sure everyone does their jobs correctly.

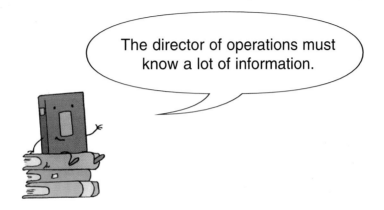

The director of operations must know a lot of information.

CLICK. CLICK.

Office people work for big trucking companies, too. They take care of bills, paychecks, schedules, and other important things.

CLICK! CLANK! CLUNK!

Maintenance workers check to see that the trucks are in good shape and ready to go.

Diesel mechanics work on the engines of big trucks.

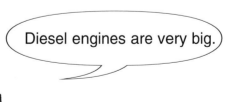

Diesel engines are very big.

TINK! CLATTER!

Truck drivers also check the trucks they will be driving. They don't want to get stuck on the road in a broken-down truck! Truck drivers are very careful people.

Truck drivers must know a lot about their trucks before they drive them.

VROOM! VROOM!

And there goes a truck—off to a city 100 miles away.

GLOSSARY

common carrier (KAH–mun KA–ree-ur)
A common carrier is a trucking company that moves things from one place to another. Common carriers deliver many different things.

dispatcher (dis–PAT–chur)
The dispatcher is the person who tells the truck drivers which trucks to drive.

freight (FRAYT)
Freight is another word for things a trucking company moves from place to place.

mechanic (meh–KA–nik)
The mechanic is the person who fixes the trucks.

terminal (TER–mih–null)
The terminal is the building where truck drivers pick up and drop off goods. Some terminals are very large.

INDEX

CAROLE GREENE has published over 200 books for children. She also likes to read books, make teddy bears, work in her garden, and sing. Ms. Greene lives in Webster Groves, Missouri.